Doug Manning, a former pastor of several Baptist churches, is involved in full-time lecturing and writing. He heads The Family Growth Center in Hereford, Texas.

This series offers the concerned reader basic guidelines and *practical* applications of religion for today's world. Although decidedly Christian in focus and emphasis, the series embraces all denominations and modes of Bible-based relief relevant to our lives today. All volumes in the Steeple series are originals, freshly written to provide a fresh perspective on current—and yet timeless—human dilemmas. This is a series for our times. Among the books:

Woman in Despair: A Christian Guide to Self-Repair
Elizabeth Rice Handford

A Spiritual Handbook for Women
Dandi Daley Knorr

How to Read the Bible
James Fischer

Bible Solutions to Problems of Daily Living
James W. Steele

A Book of Devotions for Today's Woman
Frances Carroll

Temptation: How Christians Can Deal with It
Frances Carroll

With God on Your Side: A Guide to Finding Self-Worth Through Total Faith
Douglas Manning

*Help in Ages Past, Hope for Years to Come: Daily Devotions
from the Old Testament*
Robert L. Cate

A Daily Key for Today's Christians: 365 Key Texts of the New Testament
William E. Bowles

Walking in the Garden: Inner Peace from the Flowers of God
Paula Connor

How to Bring up Children in the Catholic Faith
Carol and David Powell

*Sex in the Bible: An Introduction to What the Scriptures
Teach Us About Sexuality*
Michael R. Cosby

*How to Talk with God Every Day of the Year: A Book of Devotions for
Twelve Positive Months*
Frances Hunter

God's Conditions for Prosperity: How to Earn the Rewards of Christian Living
Charles Hunter

Pilgrimages: A Guide to the Holy Places of Europe for Today's Traveler
Paul Lambourne Higgins

*Journey into the Light: Lessons of Pain and Joy to Renew Your Energy and
Strengthen Your Faith*
Dorris Blough Murdock

WITH GOD ON YOUR SIDE

Discovering Self-Worth Through Total Faith

Doug Manning

A SPECTRUM BOOK

Prentice-Hall, Inc. Englewood Cliffs, New Jersey 07632

Library of Congress Cataloging in Publication Data

Manning, Doug.
   With God on your side.

   (Steeple books)
   "A Spectrum Book."
   Includes index.
   1. Christian life—1960- 2. Self-respect.
I. Title. II. Series.
BV4501.2.M338 1984.   248.4   83-11064
ISBN 0-13-961474-5
ISBN 0-13-961433-8 (pbk.)

This book is available at a special discount when ordered
in bulk quantities. Contact Prentice-Hall, Inc., General
Publishing Division, Special Sales, Englewood Cliffs, N.J. 07632.

Editorial/production supervision: Suse L. Cioffi
Cover design by Hal Siegel
Manufacturing buyer: Edward J. Ellis

©1984 by Prentice-Hall, Inc., Englewood Cliffs, New Jersey 07632

A SPECTRUM BOOK

ISBN 0-13-961433-8 {PBK.}

ISBN 0-13-961474-5

2 3 4 5 6 7 8 9 10

Printed in the United States of America

Prentice-Hall International, Inc., *London*
Prentice-Hall of Australia Pty Limited, *Sydney*
Prentice-Hall of Canada Inc., *Toronto*
Prentice-Hall of India Private Limited, *New Delhi*
Prentice-Hall of Japan, Inc., *Tokyo*
Prentice-Hall of Southeast Asia Pte. Ltd., *Singapore*
Whitehall Books Limited, *Wellington, New Zealand*
Editora Prentice-Hall do Brasil Ltda., *Rio de Janeiro*

To Barbara Maddox Manning,
who has walked with me through it all.

Contents

Preface

If you have struggled with the meaning of faith . . .

If you have struggled with the purpose of your life . . .

If you have struggled with how God works . . .
this book was written for you.

This book was written by a struggler *for* strugglers. It will give an honest report of one man's journey toward meaning—the meaning of faith, the meaning of self, and the meaning of purpose.

Here you will find help for your own journey. The help will not be found in easy answers nor quick fixes. The help

will be found in a new discovery of a God who loves you—
and the slow application of that love to the issues of life.

The book is divided into three sections: Each section de-
velops a part of the whole. I hope that the sum of the
three sections will prove to be greater than the parts.

PART I: THE DISCOVERY OF LOVE

The one overriding message from God is that He loves us—
just as we are—unconditionally. We do not perform for His
love; rather, we discover His love and we're changed by the
discovery.

PART II: THE DISCOVERY OF ACCEPTANCE

Acceptance from God is the key to self-worth and is the
prerequisite for all other acceptance. Acceptance from
God is not the total acceptance we need—there must also
be acceptance from others as well as acceptance from ourselves.

PART III: DISCOVERY'S RESULTS

We do not behave a certain way in order to enter into a relationship with God. Behavior is a result of a relationship
with God rather than a relationship with God being the re-

sult of behavior. Love and acceptance produce self-worth. Self-worth affects our lives in the areas of anger, lust, selfishness, and stress. These areas change, not because of our efforts, but rather because of the changes in our needs.

ACKNOWLEDGMENTS

This book could not have been written without the help of a group of folks who have affected my life: the late Grady Nutt, who was a friend and an encourager; Mary Kennan, Acquisition Editor, General Publishing Division, who had the first dream; Carolyn Baxter, who typed, edited, and gave hope; and Lynton and Joyce Allred, who have always believed in me.

part one

THE DISCOVERY
OF LOVE

Sometimes I wish we could start
all over with our faith.
Throw out all of the comfortable
slogans and theological jargon,
And discover a new way to
put verbs to our faith.

chapter one

Who Will Answer?

In the canyons of the mind we wander on and
stumble blindly
Through the often tangled maze of starless
nights and sunless days,
While asking for some kind of clue—a road
to lead us to the truth.
But—who will answer?[1]

We Christians would rather flippantly respond, "Christ, Christ is the answer. He is the way out of every difficulty. Just 'Turn it over to Him, and all will be well.'"

Having said it, we lean back in our smugness with complete assurance in our answer. Then someone says, "How does He answer?" and our smugness is gone.

How does Christ answer? What does He answer? How does religion work in the human life? What can faith cure? What are its limitations? All of these questions are issues. All of these issues are in the one question, "How? How does Christ answer?"

HOW DOES CHRIST ANSWER?

I have spent 30 years in the ministry either trying to answer this question or trying to avoid answering it. I must confess that I have spent more time avoiding than answering. Looking back over the pile of sermons I have collected in these years, I am ashamed of the methods I have used to answer or avoid the "How." Far too often my answer was some worn-out cliché which I did not understand myself, but which seemed to serve the purpose at the time. Most of the time the cliché answered nothing, but sounded so religious that the questioner seemed to accept the statement as fact even if it did nothing to clear up the issue.

I wish I could go back to all of those at whom I have thrown clichés and say, "I know I said pray about it, or just trust God, or turn it all over to Jesus, but, frankly, that was just so much talk on my part. Now let's forget the theological jargon and face the 'How He answers.'"

Clichés in Religion

I have often wondered why clichés are so popular in religion. It may be that we think religion is not supposed to make sense or be understood, or it may be that we do not *want* to understand it. If it *is* understood, it seems to lose some of its mystery and becomes commonplace.

I think it works like the story of the emperor's new clothes. A tailor was called to make a new suit for the emperor.

The tailor had, in fact, made no suit, but told the emperor he had made a suit so brilliant that only the brilliant could see it. No one wanted to admit that he was not brilliant enough to see the clothes, so no one would admit that the emperor was parading around in his birthday suit.

When we state our mystical jargon, it seems to make sense to us and so, in turn, others feel compelled to act as if it makes sense to them, also. The result is we all walk around acting as if we have found the secret to all knowledge, when all we have is a rather large repertoire of holy-sounding clichés. Unfortunately, the emperor paraded before a small boy who blurted out, "The emperor ain't got nothing on." Small boys do not play the same games as small adults. The spell was broken, and soon the whole kingdom was chanting, "The emperor ain't got nothing on."

The Church's Role Today

The church is currently playing "the emperor's new clothes game" with a vengeance unparalleled in history. The television, the radio, and the pulpits are crammed with people proclaiming a theological answer for every question and a religious cure for every problem. Accompanied by the appropriate number of "Praise Gods" and "Hallelujahs," we are bombarded with a theology which is more closely related to motivational seminars than to the Bible. The gospel according to this theological mumbo jumbo is "everyone can be happy all of the time." No one should be sick, or poor, or worried, or unhappy. The theme seems to be "if we get right with God, we have every problem permanently solved."

Unfortunately, we are hearing only one side of the story. These folks tell us their successes, but we do not hear of their failures. The result of this approach is that masses of people feel compelled to testify to cures they have never found, healing they have never experienced, and blessings they have never felt.

The Church Seen in Reality

I am no prophet, but I *will* make a prediction. The day will come when this bubble will burst. Just like the little boy who blew the emperor's cover, people will begin to look at themselves and say, "I ain't got nothing on." When it begins to blow, the church will be in for its roughest day ever: Christians may become the laughingstock of society. In our zeal to sell the gospel, we have ignored too much nakedness and too many problems. We have been content to act as if we have found answers that we have not actually found. The result may well be disastrous.

Games Christians Play

When I was not playing the game of clichés, I had some other weapons in my arsenal. One of the best was what I now call the "don't do that" approach.

The "Don't Do That" Approach. This game is played by simply finding a text and proclaiming with great authority that we, as Christians, are just not supposed to do it. A good example would be the text in Matthew 6:25-34:

> 25. Therefore I bid you put away anxious thoughts about food and drink to keep you alive, and clothes to cover your body. Surely life is more than food, the body more than clothes.
>
> 26. Look at the birds of the air; they do not sow and reap and store in barns, yet your heavenly Father feeds them. You are worth more than the birds!
>
> 27. Is there a man of you who by anxious thoughts can add a foot to his height?
>
> 28. And why be anxious about clothes? Consider how the lilies grow in the fields; they do not work, they do not spin;
>
> 29. And yet, I tell you, even Solomon in all his splendour was not attired like one of these.
>
> 30. But if that is how God clothes the grass in the fields, which is there today, and tomorrow is thrown on the stove, will He not all the more clothe you? How little faith you have!
>
> 31. No, do not ask anxiously, "What are we to eat? What are we to drink? What shall we wear?
>
> 32. All these are things for the heathen to run after, not for you, because your heavenly Father knows that you need them all.

33. Set your mind on God's kingdom and his justice before everything else, and all the rest will come to you as well.

34. So do not be anxious about tomorrow; tomorrow will look after itself. Each day has troubles enough of its own.[2]

The "don't do that" approach simply expounds on this text and says: We are not supposed to worry. If we worry, we are sinning. At no time do we try to answer *how* we are to stop worrying. At no time do we deal with the root causes of worry. We just say, "Stop it," and that takes care of that.

Guilt and Fear in Religion

If the clichés and the "don't do it" approach failed, I could always depend on the old faithful twins of fear and guilt. "God will get you if you do" covers the fear end. "God will get you if you don't" takes care of the guilt. When I look back on my sermons in recent years, I am appalled at how often I used the terrible twins to motivate the folks who came to hear me.

Need for the "Terrible Twins." I am even more appalled at how effective the twins were. We seem to have a need

[2] *The New English Bible*, Oxford University Press and Cambridge University Press, 1961

for guilt and fear in religion. If a sermon is preached without at least one of these, we do not feel as if we have been to church. A great deal of the feelings we attribute to the presence of the Holy Spirit are actually the grip of fear and guilt making a hurting in the chest which we interpret as the presence of God.

The Five Easy Steps

When I began to move away from the methods of clichés, guilt, and fear, I seemed lost. I was searching for answers. I was desperate for something to say. This brought on my "five easy steps" period. I worked every issue down to a set number of steps. I had the whole Christian life boiled down to a set of simple plans. Salvation was four spiritual laws and the Christian walk was seven easy keys. I am sure I became the most obnoxious of preachers with my bad case of the "simples." I had worked out a new version of the old emperor's new clothes game.

There came a time in my life when I had to face my own nakedness. The clichés could no longer be tolerated. I was tired of telling myself to stop worrying, to quit getting angry, or to watch out for lust. Fear and guilt were no help at all—I had enough fear and guilt to create a saint. If these were so effective, why was I not already a saint? My "Five easy steps" were no longer easy; nor were they steps.

I seemed to have two choices: I could either find out what Christ answered and how He answered it, or I could give up. I could not make it work; in fact, I did not know *any-one* who was making it work. The whole of the Gospel had become a collection of pleasant-sounding phrases which did nothing to help me meet life. This Emperor had nothing on . . .

CHRIST AND THE MAJOR ISSUES

If Christ is to be the answer, He must meet the basic needs we all have. There must be the facing of *how* He answers. How do we deal with worry? How do we deal with anger? What can be done about lust? How does Christ help us deal with stress? What makes us become less selfish? How do value systems change? This is the stuff life is made of.

In practical terms, how does Christ handle these issues? It is evident they will not be handled by clichés, nor by fear and guilt; nor will they be preached away.

It is not enough to just say, "Stop it," even if we can quote a text to back it up. It is only enough when we can also say, "This is *how* He can help us stop it." Then, and only then we can say, "Christ is the answer."

chapter two

If Christ Is the Answer, What Is the Question?

> Don't tell me to love—
>   tell me how to love.
> Don't tell me I should love—
>   tell me how to love.
> Don't tell me I am not loving—
>   love me and let me learn.

There was a period in my life when I would not preach about love. It was not that I did not believe in love; it was not that I thought the issue was too soft, or that people needed the harder stuff of the gospel. I would not speak of love because I did not have the third point for the sermon. All sermons are supposed to have three points and a poem. I had the first two points loaded and ready.

THE THREE POINTS OF A SERMON

The first point was "We are supposed to love." I had plenty of scriptures to quote as proof of this point. Jesus even commanded us to love—He called it a new commandment that we love one another.

The second point was "We aren't loving enough." The whole world could be used as proof of this point. War, greed, lust, or any other event or attitude is ready proof that the world needs love—no, the world needs *lovers*, and there aren't many lovers around.

The third point should have been "How do we begin to love?" That is where I struck out. How does love happen in us? How do we start? What are the causes of love?

Frankly, I did not know. I found it difficult to love others and could not fathom how to become a lover. I was face to face with the issue of the first chapter in this book: It is not enough to say "do it" unless you can also say *"how* to do it."

The Third Point:
How Do We Begin to Love?

How do we become lovers? Is there a formula we work? I tried every plan I could find. One plan said to cast out all negative thoughts while shaving in the morning. While casting out the thoughts I cut myself, could not find the styptic pencil, went to breakfast with tissue stuck on the wound, and felt very little love left. If there *is* a magic formula for becoming a lover, I have never found it; and believe me, I have looked.

Facts Versus Formulas. I finally discovered a fact; not a formula. We cannot love others until we love ourselves.

Jesus knew this and told us to love our neighbor *as we love ourselves.* The way we relate to others is directly connected to how we see ourselves. If we feel down, we cannot stand for anyone else to be up. A friend of mine who is a psychologist says, "Hurt people hurt people." If we feel hated, we find it hard to love. If we feel loved, it is hard to hate.

If Christ is to answer the need of love within us, then He must help us love ourselves first. It is not enough that He encourages us to love; nor is it enough that He commands us to love. He must first make us feel love within ourselves before we can show love outside ourselves.

THE IMPORTANCE OF SELF-WORTH

The gospel must work in the area of self-esteem or self-worth if it is to effectively change us. To say we need self-worth is not a startling statement. A trip to any bookstore will reveal this overwhelming need immediately. The shelves are full of books on the subject, many of which have been best sellers. There is a tremendous interest in this area because it has become evident this subject is vital to human fulfillment.

Achieving Self-Worth. All of us are looking for self-worth. This seems to be the very basic need of our lives. We are born with a vacuum inside of us. The vacuum represents the need of worth, and this need dominates us until it is filled. We spend our lives trying to find something or someone who can fill the vacuum. Most of the time we try to fill it from the outside: We collect friends, compliments, toys, position, or power, trying desperately to finally prove that we are worthy people. Unfortunately, it is easier to prove our worth to others than it is to prove it to ourselves. Others see only the external part of us—they see the things we own or the position we hold, and decide we are worthy. *We* see the inside with its insecurities and fears, and continue to feel unworthy.

Inner Feelings of Self-Worth

It does not help for others to think we are worthy if we do not feel it ourselves. If I feel ugly, the whole world can say I am pretty, and it will be of little help. If I feel dumb, no one can prove I am smart. If I feel worthless, someone can tell me of my value every hour on the hour, and I will feel worthy only while he is telling me. The rest of the time I am back to square one.

The efforts of others can even become a source of anger. For example, suppose I worked for a bank and was embezzling money from them without their knowledge. Then suppose the bank gave a dinner in my honor to celebrate an anniversary of employment. The speakers would wax long and eloquent about me and my service. I would be sitting there saying to myself, "Yes, but if you *really* knew me you would not say that." Before long I would be a basket case of frustration and anger. We need worth, but it must be *self-worth* if it is to be effective.

As long as the vacuum is there, we cannot stop our constant quest for the feelings of self-worth. This is more a survival issue than an act of selfishness. The vacuum dominates us until we can think only of where we are and how we are seen.

Effects of the Vacuum

In the vacuum-dominated mode I relate to others by wondering how they feel about me instead of how I feel about them. My whole world is wrapped up in wondering if people like me, and I will do anything to earn their approval. I never think of others and their needs. I seem to approach the whole world with the plaintive cry, "How do you like me so far?"

The result of this approach is that the most feared people in the world to me are the people called "they." I must constantly worry about what "they" think. I must dress to impress "them." I must live the way "they" expect me to live. I am not free to be me. I am the product of the pressures around me rather than the person of my own choices and preferences.

The vacuum turns me into a nice conforming person with a terrific ego problem. I cannot forget about myself long enough to notice anyone else. I cannot accept others because I am too busy competing with them.

19

Filling the Vacuum

If the vacuum can begin to be filled, the difference is miraculous. If I can feel worth in myself, I no longer need others to prove it for me. If I am worthy, I do not need others with the same degree of desperation as before. Since I do not need them, I can stop worrying about how they see *me* and begin to notice *them*.

I have found my own self-worth and can begin to turn outward to others. I am no longer threatened by people because I no longer must compete with them for my position. The result is a dramatic change in me which brings out a more healthy me.

A Formula for Finding Self-Worth

The big question is, How do we fill the vacuum? How do we find self-worth? Just as in the "how to love" question, we face a dilemma. Is there a formula we follow to produce self-worth? There have been many formulas written, but very few seem to work.

Many of the successful formulas take the form of mental gymnastics. We must psych ourselves into positive thinking. This method seems to work for those who do not need much help. For those with deep-rooted inferiority complexes and chronic insecurity, "psyching themselves" tends to worsen the problem: These folks try it and fail, and as the failure deepens, so does their sense of worthlessness.

I led a study on a book about self-worth. This book did a great job in outlining the problem of low self-esteem and describing the effects of the problem. It helped us go back to our childhood and discover how we were programmed to think negatively about ourselves. Then the book stopped. The participants were frustrated and demanded to know what they were to do next. We had found the problem—now we needed the next step. To me, this next step is God.

God Fills the Vacuum

Let's say I am a person who lacks self-worth. The vacuum is inside of me and dominates all that I think or do. I need worth, but cannot seem to find any way out of the depression I feel. What if God—the being of ultimate worth—came into my life and said, "You are worthy to me. I created you on purpose, and I am pleased with what I made. I love you." If that could happen and I could accept it, not just intellectually but also emotionally, I think it would make a profound difference. If God likes me, then I can dare to like myself. If I dare to like myself, the vacuum can begin to fill and I can begin to feel self-worth. If I know that God likes me and *I* like me, then if others do not like me, *they* have a problem. In other words, if the general likes me, I don't have to worry about the corporals. I no longer fear, and I no longer desperately need the approval of others—I can be me in the midst of pressure to conform.

THE GOOD NEWS

This is how God works. This is the power of the gospel. He came to make us feel loved and to let that love make us feel worthy. The victory in Jesus is self-worth out of which everything else comes.

The question is, How do we discover this love? How do we accept it emotionally and let it become a part of our lives? How do we get comfortable with a God who loves us?

chapter three

I Fell Into Grace

When Jesus said we were to be like
little children,
Did He mean naive and dumb
or did He mean simple and uncomplicated?

He came to my office on three occasions. Each time he was too upset for the size and type of problem he brought. I was a young pastor with no intention of becoming a counselor. I could not understand why people kept coming to me with their problems. I wanted to deal with spiritual matters only, but they kept coming to me with their marriage struggles, business problems, or personal feelings of inadequacy. Every time someone came through the door, I panicked. I felt inadequate to solve my own problems, much less their problems. I was in fear that they would expose my inadequacy and my ignorance. I learned to give them a scripture, a prayer, and a pat on the head. The game was to get them out of my office as quickly as possible without their knowing the depths of the ignorance they had come to see.

This young man was put through the process three times. The problem he presented was spiritual in nature, but I had no answer beyond the usual "pray about it and turn it over to God." One Friday night the young man went home and murdered his wife. Nothing before or since has ever had the effect on my life like that Friday night. I had been given three chances and missed.

THE SPIRITUAL REACH

I was determined that I would not miss many more folks as badly as I missed that young man. I began to study the process of human life. I was like a drowning man finding a lifeboat. I grasped for knowledge with an almost insatiable appetite.

The funny thing is that as I studied people, I also studied myself. The deeper I delved into the psychological process, the more disturbed I became about the person I was and the reasons for my being this person. In this process I found out a great deal more than I wanted to know.

Dealing with an Inferiority Complex

I was the middle child of three boys. My life was a fairly normal one with very little trauma. Somehow I came out of this fairly normal life with a fair-sized inferiority complex.

Some of the causes for feeling inferior I know; some I will probably never figure out. One of the causes of my inferiority complex came from innocent teasing. My mother's family lived in our town. They were a delightful bunch of fun lovers who could carry teasing to a fine science. The tease they put on me had to do with how I looked when I was born. My older brother must have been the prettiest baby God ever made, and I must have been the ugliest. Every time the family got together, I had to hear how beautiful a baby my brother was and how ugly I was. No one ever told me that I outgrew my ugliness, if I did. This was a lovely family who would not hurt me for the world. They had no idea they were instilling the notion deep inside me that I was ugly.

The second cause of my inferiority complex generated from the first. Since I thought I was ugly, it was easy to notice all of my other flaws. Once persons begin to struggle, they tend to turn inward and self-examine themselves into inferiority. I was 6'3" tall in high school and weighed 148 pounds. I had an older brother who was an all-state football player and a younger brother who was an impressive athlete. I was a terrible athlete: The only athletic ability I had was that I could recognize pain immediately.

I entered the ministry in order to please my father. I thought that would cause him to be as proud of me as he was of my two brothers. I am sure my father was proud of me, but people who feel inferior are rarely able to feel love and acceptance.

The Effects of Anger

The inferiority, the struggle, and the defeats left me with enough inner anger to forge me into being a good firebrand preacher. I did not love others and I did not love myself. I did not love God—I *feared* God. I worked to get Him to love me, but I did not love Him.

This anger period produced a hard preacher who was fighting for his life under the guise of fighting sin. I worked at my job. I would get up early to pray, usually falling asleep on my knees and then waking with aching knees and a guilt trip. I fought to rid my mind of sexual thoughts, and I failed.

A Struggle Against Failure

One week in the late 1960s I hit the bottom. A series of events seemed to hit all at the same time. It seemed that the people I believed in the most were falling apart. Two minister friends left their wives for other women. A person I thought to be a great Christian was caught embezzling. Then one day a woman grabbed me and kissed me in my office. I wanted to have sex with her right there on the rug of my office. I did not do so, but the fact that I wanted to was more than I could bear.

I gave up. I had worked, I had prayed; I had lived the Christian life as well as I could, and, frankly, I could not make it work. I did not know anyone else who was making it work, either. I decided there was nothing to it—it was a beautiful idea, but it just did not work.

Pain as a Cure. Fortunately, the studying I had been doing stood with me in good stead. I began to take my theology apart, and I began to take myself apart. It was a painful time. I learned things I did not want to know, and I often thought I would die from the sheer weight of it all. It was a case of pain being the cure for me. This period changed my life. I often say, "I fell into grace."

I finally decided that the only place faith had to work was in me. If faith worked there I had something to say, no matter who else failed. If faith did not work there, I had nothing to say no matter who else succeeded.

Discovering a Parallel. I began to struggle with how to make this faith work in me. Gradually I began to make some discoveries. I discovered I had spent my whole life trying to convince my father to like me. I felt life would never be complete until I could feel assured of the love and acceptance of my father. I also discovered I was relating to God in the same way I related to my father. Just as I had lived in a desperate system of trying to earn my father's love, I was now living the same system of trying to earn the love and acceptance of God.

Since I always felt my father loved my brothers more than he loved me, it was natural to think God loved others more than me. These feelings caused me to redouble my efforts, only to fail again. I was in a constant state of frustration. Everything became a test of His love: If I preached and there was no response, I concluded that God had rejected me again; if I had bad thoughts, it proved how bad I was and how God was withholding His power.

HOW DO WE GET GOD TO LOVE US?

If others preached and were successful, I was deeply hurt— God loved them more than me. I could not relate to others because of my need to compete with them. I could not love others because I needed them to be down and unblessed just as I was. The result of these feelings was anger and frustration. I preached about a life more abundant, but I lived life as a basket case.

One day I began to wonder how I could ever please God. What would I have to do or be to make Him happy with me? I was willing to do about anything if I just knew what it would take. I began to ask, "How do I get God to like me?" Behave? Perform? Give? Cure? Pray? How? How? How?

I bumped into Romans 5:8:

> Christ died for us while we were
> yet sinners, and that is God's own
> proof of His love towards us.[3]

---

[3] *The New English Bible*, Oxford University Press and Cambridge University Press, 1961.

And I fell into Grace. I began with the fact that God loved me long before I performed or behaved or prayed or preached or was even a follower, and slowly I rebuilt my theology.

I do not have as much theology as I once had. What I *do* have I now enjoy. I am a simple fan of Jesus Christ. I want to be like Him. The small ways that I am like Him came from the basic truth of my theology. This truth is "God loves me." He doesn't love my behavior—He loves me. All else comes from this one basic truth. The victory in Jesus is self-worth out of which everything else comes. The self-worth comes from the discovery that I am loved.

chapter four

How to Get God to Like You

If the thought of the love of God
is more than we can fathom,
How will we ever get to the bottom
of the fact that God likes us?

How do you get God to like you? That may sound like a strange question, but it is one we are all trying to either answer or avoid. Most of the time our answers are found in some system of behavior.

I asked a youth group, "How do you get God to like you," and they could not relate to the question. I then asked them, "How do you get God *not* to like you." The answers were amazing. Such vital things were suggested as staying home from church on Sunday night to watch television, not reading the Bible, not praying, going to places He disapproves of, using language He disapproves of, or not witnessing.

Answers like this make God a "petty is as petty does" sort of God. Behave and He likes you; misbehave and He is mad. It is easy to think He loves the world, but it is very hard to believe He loves me; it is easy to believe He likes others, but it is very hard to believe He likes me.

WHO IS GOD?

Most of the time we feel God is a picky, demanding God who is never satisfied with where we are or what we have done. We see God like the football coach at Nebraska State. Several years ago his team was ahead of Oklahoma State (45-0 at the half). The coach said that being so far ahead was a hard thing for him to face. What was there to jump on the players about! That is how we see God. Whatever we have done, it is not enough—we could do better. The result is we struggle with God, while deriving very little enjoyment from the experience.

Our Relationship with God

Someone needs to say that God is not that all-fired crazy about behavior. He did not come into the world to get us to behave ourselves. He did not send Jesus to be the world's party-pooper. The key word in the New Testament is not behavior, it is *relationship*. He came to relate to us. That relationship is based on His love, not our behavior. We do not behave our way into a relationship with Him— Behavior is the result of a relationship with God, rather than a relationship with God being the result of behavior.

The good news is that we do not get God to like us, but we discover that He *already* likes us. He died for us while we were still sinners—long before we behaved. I hope we can grasp this. I think it is the most life-changing idea the world has ever known.

GOD LIKES US—NOT HOW WE BEHAVE

I once saw grace as God's unmerited favor. This is true, but it is equally true that grace means God found something about me to love. He made me and sees me as a person of worth. Like the little boy said, "I am me, and I am good 'cause God don't make no junk."

Grace and a Cinderella Story

The greatest definition of grace I have ever found is in a little book called *Being Me or Self, You Bug Me* by Grady Nutt. Grady said grace is like Cinderella the morning after the ball. She is back in the basement scrubbing floors, while upstairs her sisters are trying to get their fat feet into the slipper. Cinderella wants to run to her prince, but she knows that he fell in love with a myth. He would not love a char girl. She hears him begin to leave, and her heart breaks. He stops at the door and asks, "Are there any other girls here?" The stepmother says, "There is a char girl in the basement, but—" "Bring her here!"

Cinderella starts up the stairs, desperately trying to straighten her dress, fix her hair, and hide her fingernails.

Grady said, "Grace is God kneeling in front of us with a glass slipper in His hand—seeing potential in us that we do not even see in ourselves." He sees value in us never seen by anyone, including ourselves.[1]

The real question of religion is: Has He ever put the slipper on my foot? Has there been a time of discovery when I discovered God likes me just as I am?

I preached for years before I ever let Him slipper me. Those years were spent trying to impress Him, trying to earn His love, trying to get Him over His anger when I did not know why He was mad.

A Discovery of Love

When I finally hit bottom and had to quit trying, I finally discovered love for the first time in my life. This was not a big-time religious experience. It did not happen with a great deal of emotion and a public confession. It did not happen suddenly; instead, it was a gradual growing acceptance of the love of God. It started as an intellectual acceptance and became an emotional reality in two years' time. It has changed my life.

Misbehaving. It is important to discover that He likes us, and that He likes us all of the time. It is easy to know He

[1] Grady Nutt, *Being Me or Self, You Bug Me* (Nashville: Broadman Press, 1971), pp. 39-45. All rights reserved. Used by permission.

likes us while we are in church and behaving ourselves. But how does He feel when we are blowing it?

Peter wanted to walk on water. He saw Jesus doing it, and Peter was an impetuous man. When he asked if he could do the same, Jesus said, "Come on." Imagine what went on in the mind of Jesus during this experience. Would He think, "Look at that—Peter is walking on the water. I love him so much. Think of the witnesses. Think of what the folks on the shore will receive from this evidence of my power. Uh-oh. I spoke too soon. Look at him—he is sinking. How dare he embarrass me. What of his witness? I hope he drowns!"

That is so farfetched it is humorous. Jesus would never say, "I hope he drowns." Not about Peter!

Much of our concept and much of the preaching we hear say that that is exactly what Jesus would say. He loves us when we are good witnesses, He loves us when we perform, He loves us when we behave. But when we blow it, He rejects us. His Holy Spirit will not have anything to do with us, His blessings are withheld from us, we are unloved until we walk again.

This concept makes being a follower a constant source of pressure. We are under the gun all of the time. His love for us depends on our performance for Him.

It is easy to think He loved Peter when he was walking and He loved him when he sank. It is hard to believe the same thing about us. Most of the time we think He loved us until we sank, and then stopped loving us. The good news is He loves us *all* of the time.

GOD LOVES UNCONDITIONALLY

Grasping the concepts of "He loves *us*—not how we behave, but us, and He loves us all of the time" happens to be revolutionary. As a matter of fact, these simple concepts can change a life. When they become real, they begin to fill the vacuum of self-esteem in us. Nothing I have ever found can fill the vacuum like the discovery of the fact that God likes us. I think real self-worth begins with God.

The last section of this book deals with the profound change these simple concepts can bring into a life. Changes in anger, lust, greed, and relationships come from these concepts being a part of us.

Several years ago a friend of mine said, "I am tired of being a God pleaser. I am tired of trying to earn His love. I am just going to be me and let Him decide for Himself whether or not He loves me." I was horrified at the statement. It sounded like blasphemy, until I discovered He loves us, not how we perform or behave. Now I agree with my friend. We can be ourselves and let Him decide. We can also know how He will decide. Somehow He will find a way to love us just the way we are. I now relax and sing:

Jesus loves me, this I know,
For the Bible tells me so.
Little ones to Him belong,
They are weak, but He is strong.
Yes, Jesus loves me.
Yes, Jesus loves me.
Yes, Jesus loves me.
The Bible tells me so.

part two

THE DISCOVERY
OF ACCEPTANCE

chapter five

The God
Who Has Been There

Changing the world takes both experience
and modelling.
Don't tell me what you believe;
tell me where you have been.
Don't tell me how I should live;
show me how you are doing it.

Jesus was working in the carpenter shop. He was in a hurry. The rich lady in town had ordered a chair which was to be ready that afternoon. (Now when the rich lady orders a chair, you get it ready.) That morning, as He was attaching the last rung to the chair, He hit one too many blows with the hammer, and the rung split. This put Him behind in His work, and He would have to work fast in order to finish the chair. In His haste He became careless and brought the hammer down squarely on His thumb. And He said . . . .

By the way, what do *you* think He said?

"Verily, verily, I strucketh my thumb."
"Holy, holy, holy. God is good."

How about, "Damn it." (Or the King James equivalent thereof.)

Don't be horrified. It matters what we *think* He said. How we answer this reveals how we see Him. It is easy to see Him as God. It is hard to see Him as human. It is easy to see Jesus looking at a throbbing thumb and saying, "Be healed." It is hard to see Him jumping around a carpenter shop in pain.

SEEING JESUS AS GOD *AND* AS A MAN

It is important to see Jesus as God; it is of equal importance to see Him as a man. Seeing Him as God leads us to worship and seeing Him as a man allows us to relate to Him.

There is a text in the book of Ezekiel (Ez. 3:15) that sums up the importance of Jesus's manhood.

Ezekiel was a prophet, but he was *more* than a prophet. He was the Will Rogers of his day, except he wasn't funny. When Will was alive he served as the comforter of the nation. For example, if a disaster happened, Will would hop the next plane to be on the scene. His arrival always seemed to lessen the tragedy, although he did not really do much. When the word spread that Will was in town, somehow folks felt better.

Ezekiel was like that. The Jewish nation had been carried into Babylonian captivity. They were lonely, separated from their beloved land, and convinced they could not worship

God in a far country. Ezekiel said, "I went there, and I sat where they sat."

Jesus came to be God among us. He also came to sit where we sit. He came to experience what we experience, and He did. I used to say He experienced everything we experience, except sin. That sounded good until I was confronted with the fact that He never experienced old age or being a woman. Now I have to say He experienced the basic emotions of us all.

He knew what it was to be poor. He knew how it felt to lose a father at an early age. He knew what it was to be a member of a minority race.

He knew what it was to grow up. Our concept is that He woke up one morning and said, "I'm thirty—let's go to the river." We have a hard time grasping His growing up with all of the fears and emotions that accompany the process.

Jesus was born in a small town, and His birth was suspect. We know He was born of a virgin, but the little old ladies in the town counted the months. The men of the town called Him a bastard. I have always wondered what happened when Mary came home to tell her parents she was pregnant and the Holy Spirit did it. "The holy Who?" her father must have screamed, while her mother cried.

Jesus's growing up was real. Somewhere He learned about life. We do not know about turning the other cheek until someone has slapped us on one cheek. We do not learn about the second mile unless some Roman centurion has forced us to carry his pack the first mile.

We see Jesus as the perfect specimen in every way. We assume that He did not know what it was like to have acne or to be unathletic. Isaiah said it in Biblical terms: "He hath no form or comeliness and no beauty that we should desire Him." Uglies of the world, take heart—He has been there. He sat where you sit.

Jesus knew what it was to have trouble with His mother. Mary was and is a saint in our eyes, but she was also a typical Jewish mother: When He was 30 years old she was still trying to tell Him how to behave at weddings. He had to cut the cords from mom just the way we do—and His may have been even harder to cut.

He knew what it was like to be hungry, afraid, lonely, rejected, misunderstood, and betrayed.

He knew what it was to have sexual urges to deal with. He was tempted sexually just the way we are. (If you have trouble believing this, let some woman wash your feet with her tears, pour perfume on them, and dry them with her hair, and see if that experience is not erotic.)

He has been there. He sat where we sit. That means we can relate to Him as a person. It also means He can relate to us. He understands what we experience, and He also understands the effects of those experiences.

We are the product of what we have been through: the experiences, the raising, the griefs, the hurts, the rejections—they all go together to make us who we are. He not only understands how we are, He understands *why* we are. His acceptance of us is based on this understanding.

BECOMING A CHRISTIAN

Christianity is harder for some people than it is for others. Some of us were born with a holy spoon in our mouths, others have had to walk through hell to get anywhere. It has been easy for me—I had loving parents. I have not had soul-wrenching tragedy in my life. I have never had to live through a broken home or a drunken, abusive father who beat me. I have never lived in a ghetto with soul-killing poverty. I have not had any experience that left me angry at the whole world.

The Quaker Questions

Over the years I have asked a series of questions called the Quaker Questions. These questions lead a group from personal worth to emotional warmth, and then to spiritual warmth.

> The first question is: Where did you live between the ages of nine and twelve? How many children were in the home? Which child were you?
> The second question is: How was your home heated? (The folks began to get nostalgic at this question.)

The third question is: Where was the center of warmth in the home?

The fourth question is: Who was the person of warmth in your home?

The fifth question is: When, if ever, did God become a person of warmth to you?

The strange thing is when the people have answered the fourth question, I can answer the fifth one for them and never miss. Sometimes they have said there was no person of warmth in their home, or as a fellow from West Virginia said, "The only thing warm in my home was a pet chicken." If they answer the fourth question with a negative answer, the answer to the fifth question will be, "He never has."

We relate to God out of where we have been. A person who has never felt loved will find love hard to give and even harder to accept. A person who has never felt secure will find faith a strange thing to accept. If a person feels hated, they find it hard to love. If they feel loved, it is hard to hate.

The heroes of the faith are not those who are now the highest in spiritual attainment. The heroes are the ones who have traveled the greatest distance to get there.

Jesus sat where we sit, which means He understands all of this. He knows where we are and why we are there, and loves us any way. He meets us where we are and walks with us from there. Christianity is addition, not subtraction. He adds Himself to us. He does not take away all that we are or all we have gone through.

It is important for us to grasp this truth. It is in the grasping that we can begin to feel accepted by God as we are, warts and all. The first step to feeling loved and liked by God is the discovery that He understands who we are and why we are who we are.

Dealing with Feelings of Competition

Our world is almost overrun with those who make us feel like spiritual peons. There are those people who seem to have something we do not have. Unfortunately, they seem to enjoy being sure we all know they have something we do not have. The result is that even our religion produces a feeling of our not being okay. We end up having to compete in this area of our lives, and somehow never measure up. We sit in church and feel like a leisure suit in a world of tuxedos. We check each other's spiritual pulse, compare ourselves with the external show of others, and always suffer from the comparisons.

There are no comparisons to be made. Each of us is the unique combination of genes and experiences that work together to make us who we are. This combination was brought together because each of us fulfills a need in the plan of God. There is purpose.

The Purpose in Experiences

During my high school years I went through a period when I did not think I could perform sexually. This fear was a natural result of my feelings of inferiority. The fear had no basis, but it was very real to me, and very painful. I do not want to go through that again. Now I talk about this experience everywhere I go: The first time I told it I was frightened out of my wits. Now I tell it because I know that when I tell it, people will open up and talk to me. They are experiencing some of the same feelings and want to talk to someone who has been there. I walked through the experience for a purpose: God wanted someone who had been there to help others get through it.

The things we have been through also have purpose. They have affected us and will continue to affect us. I still have some sexual struggles and will always have them. The struggle left me with some scar tissue and some weaknesses, but there was purpose. There is purpose in the experiences of every person.

So here we are—the product of where we have been. If we can grasp this, we can grasp God's acceptance of us. If we can grasp His acceptance of us, then we can begin to accept ourselves. Accepting ourselves is the first step to self-worth. Did you ever notice how God put some of His choice people in funny looking bodies?

A Story About Purpose

She was fat. She always had had a struggle with her weight. Most of the time she lost the struggle. She over-compensated for her weight by being the clown—always the life of the party, always laughing. In the privacy of her life, she would clinch her fist and cry, "God, why did you make me like this?"

After college she went to graduate school and became a social worker. Her job was in New Orleans. Every day, as she went to work, she got on the expressway at the same spot. Just off the service road she would pass a small boy on the porch of a home. The boy would always wave and smile. The social worker finally decided to find out about the boy. She discovered he was crippled. He lived alone with his mother who had to work for his support. The mother was afraid to leave the child in the house because of the possibility of fire. Every day she would sit the boy on the porch with enough food and water to last until she returned from work. His whole world was the access road of an expressway. He had never seen a farm, never seen a cow, or a chicken.

The social worker made arrangements to take the boy with her. The first day she was going to take him to see a farm and a cow. She drove into the driveway and walked up on the porch. As she reached down to pick up the boy she said, "Lord, thank you, for making me big enough to lift him."

One of the "hows" is to discover His acceptance of us and His purpose for us.

chapter six

People Need People

I wonder, does God gossip?
Does He talk to other people about me?
If not, how come they always seem to know
His plan for my life?
If so, I wish He would quit it.

I was speaking for a religious focus week on a college campus. Most focus weeks have a standard format: The speaker is asked to address an assembly each day and be available for any classroom situations which may be offered. The big event is something called a "buzz session." The buzz sessions are held each night by a preacher and a layman. Usually there are enough teams of preachers and laymen to cover all of the dorms on campus. The teams are rotated so each team will visit most of the dorms during the week.

PROBLEMS IN THE BUZZ SESSIONS

There are a couple of problems with buzz sessions. First, the students do not necessarily want to be there. Some are present because they feel obligated; others are there because they happened to pass through the lobby at the wrong time and were trapped. The second problem is the format, which calls for the students to ask questions and the preacher to answer, usually with a long sermon. Most of the time the questions are what the student thinks the preacher wants to answer.

The result of these two problems is that the week is spent answering such profound questions as, "What is wrong with dancing?" or "Why should I marry within my faith?"

On this particular campus I found myself "buzzed out." I had answered the same questions every night and felt the questions were masking the real issues. On the final night I was to be in a girls' dorm. I checked with some of the girls and found that they had asked the same questions each night during the week. I did not know what would happen, but I was determined not to repeat the experiences of the previous nights. I asked the girls to sit on the floor in a large carpeted area and talked to them about the problem of trying to be relevant while posing questions to a preacher. I suggested we drop the questions and talk about what really bugged them.

THE BUZZ SESSIONS OPEN UP

For the first 20 minutes nothing happened. We dealt with boyfriends and hangnails, but no real issues. I noticed a girl sitting on the outskirts of the group. She was a very pretty, blond-haired girl with the saddest eyes I had ever seen. I remarked that she looked like someone who wanted to say something, and she said that she did have something to say.

Before she could speak further, a girl in the group said, "That's our rebel."

I said, "She does not look like a rebel."

The girl spoke again, "She is not a bad person, but she can't say no to anyone. If someone said, 'Let's jump off this building,' she would just go along and get into trouble."

Finally, we let the girl speak for herself. She said, "When I was nine years old, my mother told me she did not love me. She has been telling me that ever since. Now she is saying the same thing to my little brother, and it hurts. If your own mother does not love you, there must be something wrong with you. All of my life I have been looking for someone to love me."

The girl who first spoke suddenly looked like lights were going on in her mind as she said, "Wait a minute—that's why you are so nice. You are trying to get us to love you." She got up and went to the blond-haired girl. They embraced, and the girl said, "You don't have to try any more. I love you."

The meeting broke open. I could write a book about this session and the sessions which followed. I drove back to this campus to meet with these girls again. I wanted to see what happens when people open up to each other.

The meeting was a whirlwind of problem exchange. Everyone brought her problems and laid them on a table with the idea of exchanging. When everyone saw the problems of the rest of the group, she picked up her own and went home. During the experience, I asked the blond-haired girl if she wanted to trade places with another girl. She said, "No thanks. I will just keep my mother."

Just before we dismissed, a little energy bundle who was the leader in the group said, "I want to say something. I want to tell you what is bugging me. My father was an alcoholic. You don't know what that is like unless you have been there. You cannot imagine the fear when your mother grabs you out of the bed in the middle of the night and runs to a neighbor's house because your father is threatening to kill the whole family. You cannot imagine the pain of never having your friends visit in your own home because you are afraid of what they will find.

"My mother finally divorced my father about five years ago. She then married a man whom I thought would be just what I needed. He introduced me as his daughter, and for a while I felt good. He has turned out to be weird.

"Then I came to school and fell in love with a guy who now tells me he loves someone else. I will tell you what is bugging me. I have a sister who is a lesbian. She is a pretty girl, but she lives with a woman in the city. I will never forget my stepfather pointing his finger at me and saying, 'You are going to be a queer, just like your sister.' Now I don't think I am, and I do not want to be, but every man I have ever had anything to do with has mistreated me, and I am scared."

I do not know what the girls learned that night. I know that that particular night changed my life. I made some startling discoveries which still stay fresh in my memory.

REACHING OUT TO OTHERS

I learned that any time a group of 30 people are together, there will be about every problem known to man present in the group—no matter what kind of group, no matter the educational level nor the religious depth in the group—there will be all of the fears and frustrations known to man. The problem is, how can these fears and frustrations ever be met if there is no freedom to talk about them?

The most important thing I have learned is PEOPLE NEED PEOPLE. It sounds religious to say, "All I need is Jesus." It is neither religious nor true. The Bible is replete with the concept of bearing the burdens of one another. We are created to need the work of God in our lives and the work of God's people in our lives. This does not diminish the value of the work of God. It just acknowledges that God made us with a need for one another.

Self-Worth Comes from God and People

This book deals with the way God helps us find self-esteem. One of the ways God does this, or tries to do this, is to give us each other. It would be simple to just write about the work of God giving us self-worth. The truth is self-worth comes from God and people.

Anyone who has been in grief knows people need people. In grief it is great to pray, but it also feels good to have a warm body there to hold you and cry along with you.

Most of the time we find forgiveness from God after we find forgiveness from a significant human. I cannot enumerate the times I have dealt with people who suffered from debilitating guilt. They had prayed, they had tried all of the religious experiences, and still they were no better. When they finally told their story to me and I still loved them, then they could dare to believe that God could do the same.

Guilt and Self-Worth

Guilt can be the greatest enemy of self-worth a person can face. All the other ideas in this book can fail miserably if guilt has shut the door to any healing.

The Importance of Listening. If you are to find self-worth you must unload the guilt. This unloading will require a significant person. It is unfortunate, but these kinds of people are not plentiful. I wish I could say that almost any Christian will listen, understand, and accept. The truth is that Christians may be the least likely people to unload upon. Too often our Christian training leaves us ready to judge and preach rather than love and accept.

We must look for someone who will have a patient listening ear. The ear is the most healing part of the human anatomy. We do not need someone to preach, we need someone to listen.

My struggle toward self-esteem traces itself to some significant people who listened to me and loved me, despite my low self-esteem. It also traces itself through some significant people who saw value in me: A high school principal who, in his own gruff way, told me I had value I did not realize; and a college English professor who saw a brain in me I did not know I had, and encouraged me until I could believe I was important.

I wish I could simply give a religious formula for finding self-worth, but there is no formula. We need the discovery of the love of God in us. We need to let Him put the slipper on our foot. We will also need people who will love us unconditionally and will see value in us. We need God and we need people—He created us that way.

chapter seven

Looking for the Bruises

God, in a world full of sure-fire
formulas and quick fixes,
Looks like I could escape ever
having to be responsible for myself.

It sounds holy to say, "All I need is Jesus." It also sounds comfortable. If all I need is Jesus, then I do not have to do anything except find Him. He will do all of the rest, leaving me free to sit back and let it all happen; then I am not to blame.

One of the hardest tasks we face is assuming responsibility for ourselves. We want someone else to be responsible, to worry, to think, to make decisions, to take action, and to take the blame. This lets us off of the hook. We can be victims of our fate, cursing the results and playing "poor me" through life.

Much of current religion fits the human desire to avoid responsibility: We are to be helpless and dependent; we are to feel unable to do anything positive, and we are to assume that our thoughts and our will are wrong. From this stance of proper helplessness, God can take over and work in us. "Let go and let God" is the current concept.

The results of this concept are frustrating. We try to surrender, but can never let go completely. We try to put it all on Jesus, but can't leave it there. "Take your burden to the Lord and leave it there" is a better song title than it is a practical principle to live by. We tend to get saved and sit. No action is taken by us because none is required, and if action *were* taken, it might be seen as anti-faith. So our job is to "only believe."

What are God's Intentions?

Is God trying to make us victims? Is He trying to keep us utterly dependent? Does He want us to feel incapable of decisions, or actions, or even thoughts? The first lie the Devil told was that God wants us to be stupid. The Devil said that God knew if we ate from the tree of knowledge, we would be as smart as God. The implication is that God did not want us to be capable people, but, rather, to be stupid and dependent. Unfortunately, this first lie of the Devil has now become part of the gospel—a concept that is preached from pulpits every Sunday. Far too many sermons give the impression that the Christian is supposed to feel incompetent. If something comes from our will it is wrong. If we have a thought, it is a bad thought. If we have an idea the result of the idea will be evil. We are led to believe that God wants us to be helpless and stupid. We need to realize that Jesus died to take away our sins—not our minds.

Transferring Responsibility to God

A young nurse told me she always prays before she gives a shot to a patient. I asked her what she does when she gives a bad shot. Her answer was that she assumes her prayer was not done correctly: Either she does not say it with the right words, or she is not sincere. My response was, "God knows you can give a shot, *you* know you can give a shot—why don't you just give it? Let God get glory out of having created a competent nurse. If it were not for God, the ability, the calling, and the caring would not be there. Let His glory be in the completed project. He created a nurse."

Dependency Versus Competence. The nurse thought I was blasphemous. It sounded so much more religious to play the game of dependency. The game of competence sounded like pride and self-assuredness. The game of dependency set her up for self-hate. Every good shot came from God, every bad shot was her fault. The game also set her up for no growth. If she performed as a nurse for the rest of her life, she was never to be competent enough to give a shot without help.

DISCOVERING WISDOM AND INSIGHT

In my early days as a counselor, I depended on James 1-5 for my source of knowledge. I lacked wisdom, and James said if anyone lacks wisdom, let him ask of God. I thought the secret was to remain dumb, or at least play dumb and ask God for the insight. (Any other approach would be taking matters into my own hands, and taking matters into my own hands would be a sin and would have disastrous results.)

This proved to be a comfortable arrangement. I could remain incompetent and still get the job done. If things went bad, I could hide behind my text. I finally did a study of this text and found out my concept did not hold water. The Phillips translations of James 1:1-8 says:

> When all kinds of trials and temptations crowd into your lives, my brothers, don't resent them as friends! Realize that they come to test your faith and to produce in you the quality of endurance. But let the process go until that endurance is fully developed, and you will find you have become men of mature character with the right sort of independence. And, if in the process, any of you does not know how to meet any particular problem he has only to ask God—who gives generously to all men without making them feel foolish or guilty—and he may be quite sure that the necessary wisdom will be given him. But he must ask in sincere faith without secret

doubts as to whether he really wants God's help or not. The man who trusts God, but with inward reservations, is like a wave of the sea, carried forward by the wind one moment and driven back the next. That sort of man cannot hope to receive anything from the Lord, and the life of a man of divided loyalty will reveal instability at every turn.[1]

Suddenly, the words "right sort of independence" stuck in my mind. These words seemed to say that God was trying to make me competent, that I was to become a complete person. God was not trying to keep me stupid and dependent. The word "wisdom" in Verse 5 is the word for theoretical wisdom: A better word might be "insight." God does not give specific instructions, but He gives enough insight for my mind to work with in order to figure out the answer.

Dealing with Independent Thinking

This concept is freeing and yet frightening. It is freeing in the sense that I no longer must play dependent when I do not feel helpless. It frees me to see my own growth as part of the plan of God, to discover my own abilities and strengths, and to discover the purpose my life has on this

---

[1] *The New Testament in Modern English*, translated by J.B. Philips. New York; The MacMillan Co., 1958.

earth. Truth sets us free. This truth freed me from a prison of denying my own strength and worth.

This concept is also frightening. If God is trying to instill growth in me, then I must grow; if God is trying to develop me, then I must assume responsibility for growth. If God is not going to do it all for me, then I must do some of it for myself.

Taking Responsibility.   The life of Jesus illustrates this concept. The people He touched were made responsible. He did not walk through the world doing everything for people. Most of the people He touched were bound not only by illness, but also by hopelessness. They were victims: They had given themselves over to the idea that there was nothing they could do about their condition. Jesus cut through their dependence and made them responsible, at least in part, for their own healing.

To some He said, "Rise, take up your bed and walk." To others He said, "Your own faith will be the key." Faith in this sense was not only the ability to believe in Him, but the ability to take action. To still others He said, "Go show yourselves to the priest."

To the man at the pool He said, "Do you want to get well?" (The implication was: Are you so comfortable in your hopelessness that you do not want to change?) To the woman at the well He said, "Go get your husband." (The idea was: Let's get to the root of your hopelessness.

You have had five husbands and have become a victim of the treatment you have received. Let's face the issue.) To the rich young ruler He said, "Let's get to the root of your dependency on money. Go sell all that you have and give it away."

The list could go on. In almost every case the people were waiting for someone else to heal them. In almost every case Jesus forced them to become involved in their own healing.

HEALING AND GROWTH

Jesus is still in the business of forcing us to become involved in our own healing. The discovery of the love of God is the first great step toward healing. The help others may give is a vital part of our healing, but nothing takes the place of the struggling and the discovery we take on ourselves. Healing and growth do not come from outside sources alone, they also come from within ourselves.

Helping Ourselves. The hardest part of this struggle and discovery may well be giving ourselves permission to do so. We have been programmed to think it all must come from God. It will seem as if we are going against the faith if we begin to help ourselves—it just doesn't seem as religious. A good deal of this chapter has been spent on getting us to allay this fear, hopefully, we can now look at our part in the process of finding worth.

Finding Worth

Our part is a process called "looking for the bruises." Often we bump ourselves in the course of a day and promptly forget the bump, thinking no longer about the event. A few days later a bruise appears. We cannot remember the bumping and cannot figure out the cause of the bruise. Not knowing where the bruise came from causes consternation: We wrack our brain trying to remember. If we *can* remember, the bruise is no longer a problem.

An Analogy. The same thing happens to our psyche There have been bruises in our past. We are not born with a bad self-image; we *learn* the fine art of self-hate, a learning that comes from bad experiences in our past. It is necessary to dig these experiences out and discover the results they caused.

When bad things happen to us, we have certain thoughts, feelings, and reactions. Gradually the thoughts, feelings, and reactions separate from the event and from each other. Like a bruise they appear, but there is no known cause for their being there. We have patterns of thought, feeling, and reacting that seem natural to us because we have always thought, felt, and reacted in certain ways. The thoughts, feelings, and reactions have separated from the events; hence, they are there with no known cause. If these thoughts, feelings, and reactions can be traced back to the cause and can be *reconnected* to the cause, we will be able to deal with them in a logical manner; then we can forget them.

Tracing the Bruises

When I was young I had a great deal of inferiority feelings: I was not athletic and felt clumsy. As I grew to be an adult, the feelings were still there: I could have a hard day on the golf course and end up feeling the same way I felt in high school. I would come home in a state of depression and self-hate. After I traced the bruises, I began to understand where the feelings were coming from. I was not feeling the results of the current round of golf—I was feeling the results of all of the bruises of my youth! When I recognized the feelings for what they were, I could deal with them and go on with the day's golf game.

Tracing the bruises requires going back through life to discover the causes. We may be amazed at how simple the causes are. Mine began with the teasing I received about being an ugly baby. Others might be something just as silly as that, or they might be far more serious. The idea is to go back to the first time we felt or thought or reacted in a negative manner about ourselves.

The Discovery. When we discover the causes, we then work out the patterns and begin to recognize the recurrence of those patterns in our lives now. Basically, we are trying to find out why we feel the way we feel.

One word of caution: If the bruises are those caused by deep trauma such as child abuse, sexual abuse, alcoholism in the family, rejection by the family, or other such major abuses, you may need the help of a professional. We are the product of what we have been through. If we have been through more than what we are equipped to take, then it is necessary to take advantage of the help of others. This is no admittance of failure on our part or on God's part. If we need help, we should give ourselves permission to go get it. Life is too short for us to live miserable lives because of yesterday's bruises.

God does much to give us worth and people can help us discover that worth. Now is the time for us to rise, pick up our beds, and walk.

part three

DISCOVERY'S RESULTS

chapter eight

Self-Worth and Anger

He made me angry.
He made me furious.
I clamped down on myself. I counted
to ten. I said nothing.
A attained victory and a stomachache.

What are we supposed to do with anger? The natural response is to think we are to control it. We are brought up to think we must count to ten, pray, or just not get angry. A Christian is not supposed to be angry. But we get angry, anyway. All the prayer meetings in the world cannot stop us from feeling anger. There are things in our world that make us mad, even livid.

DEALING WITH ANGER

The simplistic cop-out is to think, "The devil made me get angry." Perhaps we are demon-possessed. The simplistic answer at this point is to try to find some religious experience to conquer the devil or to cast out the demon. When the devil is whipped and the demon gone, we still get mad.

I have a friend with a problem temper. His anger goes beyond the normal "get mad" stuff to violent rages. I have watched him search, in vain, for an answer: No one I know has had more religious experiences. He attended a charismatic meeting in Dallas, where they put him through a whole gamut of experiences: Demons were cast out, prayers were offered, and he spoke in different tongues. Speaking in different tongues encouraged him: For once in his life he was out of control without anger. Until now, anger had been the only release he could find from his usually controlled disposition. The tongues were an alternate form of releasing pent-up feelings.

He came home elated, feeling that a cure had been found. For a week, all was well. Then there came a night when the anger hit again: He was devastated. The result was a depressed man who thought there was no cure for his problem.

Christianity: A Cure for Anger

There *is* a cure for anger: It is a remedy called Christianity. This cure is not simple nor sudden, nor does it happen through an emotional religious experience.

If Christianity works, it must work in the attitude areas of our lives. It must offer some hope for areas like anger. It must first be clear that there is nothing wrong with anger. It is a natural response built into our lives. If hurt comes, the inevitable result is anger; if frustration happens, we get mad.

The greatest problem most of us have with anger is not that we express too much of it, but that we express far too little of it. Because we have been programmed from early childhood to think of anger as bad, we swallow it. Swallowed anger makes us sick: The result of swallowed anger is depression.

Depression

In counseling people, one of the main areas which must be dealt with is depression. The first question I ask is, "What do you do when you are angry, hurt, frustrated, or rejected?" The question seems to go beyond anger, but all of these feelings come from the same emotion and can be referred to as anger. It is necessary to explain the broad range of emotional responses because although some people think they never get mad, they can understand and admit to getting hurt or frustrated. Most of us are so geared into thinking anger is wrong that we cannot admit we are ever guilty of this mortal crime.

When a person understands the gamut of emotions he is dealing with when he is asked about anger, he will usually reveal that he takes no action when he gets angry. Usually he pouts or becomes quiet until the feelings go away—but the feelings do not go away. Instead, they sink into the subconscious and fester until some kind of release is necessary. This release can take the form of physical illness, the shutting off of all feelings, giving up on a relationship, an explosion of violence, or it can manifest itself as depression.

We usually think of depression as a feeling of hopelessness; however, this is only one symptom. We often do not recognize depression because we think the only symptom is a "blue" period of being down, but depression is also experiencing a loss of feelings. People gradually discover that they are living in a state of emotional blandness: Nothing matters enough to instill excitement; nothing seems to be able to stir their emotions. This depression is usually the result of swallowed anger building up until it shuts off feelings. This is the anger problem most of us have to deal with.

Allowing Ourselves to Be Angry

Dealing with pent-up anger requires:

1. *The realization that anger is natural.* It is not wrong to get mad; it is wrong to do some bad acts while we are mad, but there is nothing wrong with getting angry. Jesus got angry, and so will we. The Bible does not say, "Do not get mad." The Bible says, "Be angry and sin not." It sounds strange, but the first step in handling anger is to give ourselves permission to be angry. Healthy people get mad and do not get mad at themselves when they do so.

2. *Learning to deal with anger at the right time.* I spend a great deal of time in counseling training people how to fight. One of the greatest problems in marriages is in the spouses' learning how to express anger. Most of the time we swallow until there is an explosion or depression. Anger must be handled by saying what we feel: "That makes me angry" is one of the healthiest statements to be made in a marriage. This statement gives the spouse permission to express his/her feelings. The amazing thing is that anger expressed when it first appears will create fewer fights rather than more fights. Fights derive from swallowed anger, which builds up until there is an explosion.

The method of dealing with normal anger is to recognize it as a natural reaction and not as a sin. This avoids the fear and guilt, which are often our reactions to our anger. When anger comes, we tell ourselves we ought not to feel such feelings. Then we react further and think there is something wrong with us or we would not be experiencing these feelings. The result is we decide we are bad, or crazy, or not saved. This reaction intensifies the feelings until we become a bundle of self-loathing. If we can accept anger as a natural expression of feeling, we can allow ourselves to get mad without feeling the need of self-punishment.

After acceptance comes the ability to express feelings at the first appearance. If we wait, it builds. If it builds, we are headed for either an explosion or depression. The healthy way to deal with normal anger is to deal with it naturally. If something makes us angry, we need to say, "I am angry."

Abnormal Anger

So far we have dealt with normal anger. What about abnormal anger? What can be done with a violent temper? There are people who seem to have a hair-triggered volcano boiling inside of them. At the slightest provocation, they explode, often with no provocation at all. What can be done with this kind of anger?

The usual answer would be: Control it. But no one can control his temper. If the temper is there, it will come out no matter what we try to do to keep the lid on. The answer to this kind of temper must not deal with the temper itself, but must go *behind* the temper and deal with the cause. To treat the temper is to treat the symptom and not the disease.

Tempers and Insecurity.   People with violent tempers have them because they need them: They feel threatened, and, therefore, feel the need of defending themselves. Most of this threat comes from their own feelings of insecurity.

This feeling of insecurity can come from the hurts and angers of childhood. If a person feels hated, it is hard for that person to love, if a person feels loved, it is hard for that person to hate. The hurts of childhood can leave a person feeling threatened by life itself. This sense of threat causes people to be on guard and ready to react to any and all attacks. They need anger for defense.

The feeling of being threatened can come from being dominated most of their lives. They can feel inadequate to such a degree that the only time they can ever express any feelings is when they are angry. While angry they can explode and then blame the explosion on the anger. They need the anger to hide behind.

Controlling Temper. Controlling temper, then, must come from some method of helping people improve how they feel about themselves. If they can discover worth, value, and self-esteem, then they no longer feel the need of defense or the need to hide.

Into this very need comes the good news of a God who loves. When this good news is discovered and dealt with, then the feelings of worth and self-esteem can come forth. Out of these new feelings about ourselves comes healing for the violence we once so desperately needed.

My friend with the violent temper did not need another religious exorcism to rid him of some demon. He needed to go back to the source of his insecurity and discover why he felt so threatened. Why did he need so much defense? Why couldn't he express feelings without having to blame it on the anger? The answer is that his problem was not anger, but his own feelings of insecurity about himself.

Healing for the Normal Anger. If there is a need for dealing with anger at the right time, then there is also a need for feeling worthy enough to stand up for our feelings. Most swallowing takes place because we do not feel worthy of expressing how we feel.

What do we do with anger? We have two choices. We can try counting to ten until we blow, or we can discover our worth through the love of God and let the anger die a natural (or should I say a supernatural) death.

chapter nine

Self-Worth and Lust

Thank you, Father, for giving us such
a wonderful experience as sex.
I could not have thought of a better way
to make love.
Now, could you give me a hint about how
to think about something else occasionally?

I asked a group of young Bible scholars how religion had helped them handle lust. One young man who seemed to serve as the spokesperson for the group said, "Jesus has already won that victory for us. All we need to do is turn it over to Him. When I am tempted, I say, 'Jesus, you promised victory, so I am removing myself and claiming victory.'"

I said, "How is it working?"

He said, "Not too good. I keep forgetting to get out of the way and let Him do it."

CONTROLLING LUST

This young man is not the only one with an inadequate program for handling lust. No matter what method we use to control this monster, most of us flunk the lust test most of the time. We are often left to feel that either our methods do not work, or that they work for some but not for us. Most of us think we have more of a problem in this area than anyone else, with a result that we think something is wrong with us.

The problem is in the methods available to us for controlling this force. The only cures we know are fear and guilt. Neither of these is effective.

Methods for Controlling Lust

We should never refer to the ten laws of God as the Ten Commandments. Instead, we should call them the One Commandment and the Nine Shoulds. Our concept is that all of the commandments can be forgiven except Number Seven. If you break any of the nine, you can get over them by next Sunday. If you break old Number Seven, you are living in adultery for life.

I introduced a service one Sunday morning by saying, " I have a confession to make. You are supposed to be a forgiving community, so I want to confess it to you. I really blew it last week. I was guilty of hate." The audience reacted with a tremendous burst of apathy. I pointed this out to them and then said, "I confessed hate, and your attitude is, 'So what?' If I had confessed to adultery, I would not have a job by noon. Where does it say that adultery is worse than hate? Why is one easily overlooked and the other unforgivable? I am not saying adultery is alright—I just think we ought to get things into perspective."

The reason we have such a hangup about adultery is because we have a great fear of sex. It seems to be a powerful force which cannot be controlled. The only way we know how to control it is to keep the penalty high. If the penalty is high enough, maybe we won't do it. Perhaps, if the penalty were lowered, we would be having orgies in the streets.

Fear of Sex

One result of this fear is a great deal of guilt about all things sexual. Any sexual thought is automatically carnal. From our earliest years we were programmed to respond with guilt and shame to the normal sexual feelings inherent in us all.

Another result of fear of sex is frustration, both sexually and spiritually. On the one hand we all have sexual thoughts and feelings no matter how spiritual we are. On the other hand we seem convinced that these feelings are wrong and would not be there if we were right with God.

Most of us have spent a great part of our lives struggling with our sexuality. As Christians we have no clear view of what is right and natural about sex: All we have is our own fears and programming. The result is frustration leading to elaborate efforts to control this drive which seems more powerful than we are. Most of our control efforts are escapist in nature, such as the young man trying to get out of the way and letting God do it. Most of the efforts do not work.

How does God help us with lust? If He is to be the answer, then He must answer here. All of us face lust—more than we will ever admit. Who could we talk to about how much our mind dwells on sex? Who could we talk to about our sexual fantasies?

THERE IS A DIFFERENCE
BETWEEN TEMPTATION AND LUST

Before we can deal with lust, we must first define what lust is. There is some confusion in this area—a great deal of what we call lust is really temptation.

All of my life I have heard, "It is just as bad to think it as it is to do it." This is not so, according to the Bible. The Bible says it is just as bad to lust as it is to commit the act. The exact quote is from the Sermon on the Mount:

> You have learned that they were told, "Do not commit adultery." But what I tell you is this: If a man looks on a woman with a lustful eye, he has al-

ready committed adultery with her in his heart. Matthew 5:27-28.[1]

There must be a difference between temptation and lust. Jesus was tempted. The Hebrew writer said He was tempted in all points just as we are:

Therefore, since we have a great high priest who has passed through the heavens—Jesus, the Son of God— let us hold fast to the religion we profess. For ours is not a high priest unable to sympathize with our weaknesses—but one who, because of his likeness to us, has been tested in every way, only without sin. Let us therefore boldly approach the throne of our gracious God where we may receive mercy and find timely help in his grace. Hebrews 4:14-16.[2]

If He was tempted in all points just as we are, then He must have been tempted sexually. The Bible says He was tempted, but without sin. The conclusion must be that temptation is not sin. The Bible says that lust is sin. There must be a difference between the two.

I have defined the difference for myself. Paul often said he had no sure word of God on the subject he was writing about at the time. I am like Paul at this point—I have no

[1] *The New English Bible*, Oxford University Press and Cambridge University Press, 1961.
[2] Ibid.

sure word from God. I have been forced to face the issue and have tried to come up with a solution I can live with. It may be that each of us must come up with our own solution. All I can do is share how I see it.

To me temptation is the natural, God-given response between the sexes. There are persons whom I find sexually attractive and there are persons whom I love deeply with no sexual context in the relationship. Then there are others who seem to attract me in a sexual manner: When I see them, I have sexual thoughts, and I may be tempted by this response. I may feel this temptation to an almost overpowering depth.

I think this is normal. We are sexual beings. We think about sex because our bodies are designed with a normal and healthy sexual appetite. The body responds to sexual needs in the same natural way it responds to the need for food or water. To call this natural response "sin" or "carnal" is to relegate the body itself as evil. Just as surely as we crave food when we are hungry, we will crave sex because we are built to need both food and love.

When do we stop experiencing normal and right temptation and start lusting? The normal answer is that temptation is thinking about it—and lust is dwelling on it. My response is, "How long can you think about it before you are dwelling on it? One minute? Five minutes? An hour?" I want to know. I want to go up to the last second, but I do not want to go over the line.

Attitude

The difference between temptation and lust must be related to attitude. Temptation must be normal attraction and lust is when I move the normal attraction into an attitude of selfish gratification. If I begin to feel or say, "I must have this person no matter what the cost, no matter how much it hurts this person, no matter if it creates havoc in the person's life," then I am lusting. If I want what I see and do not care who is hurt, then I have moved into lust. I have not done the act, but the attitude is there.

Earlier in this book I told you of a young lady kissing me in my office. I was tempted. I wanted to have sex with her right there on the rug of my office. While I was feeling tempted, I was also feeling that I could not create problems for her: I knew she could not live with the results. This knowledge held me back. I have always felt that I experienced temptation which did not become lust.

The Ego

The thing that moves temptation to lust is ego need. Lust is temptation plus selfishness. People who lust are not driven by a greater need for sex than those who are just tempted. They are driven by their own needs for support, worth, or proving.

The male sex drive is often spoken of as a wild, untamable monster. It is highly overrated. This drive in a healthy person is real, but manageable; this drive in an unhealthy person becomes an all-consuming force. If ego need is added to the male sex drive, it becomes more intense.

The female sex drive is also multiplied by insecurity, the need to prove, or the lack of worth.

Most of the people who live a promiscuous lifestyle are not oversexed. They probably do not enjoy sex any more than other people. They are not doing what they do for sex: They are trying to prove something. They feel a tremendous need to conquer others, to be accepted by others, or to show others they are okay.

They have too much left to prove because they have spent their lives performing for the wrong audience. They have tried to build their worth in the eyes of others, never having concentrated on proving it to themselves. Their worth comes from outside themselves. Real worth must come from inside: If I do not think I am good, no one can make me feel good. If I do not think I am pretty, no one can make me feel pretty.

People with a lust problem do not need to learn how to control sex because sex can't be controlled. They do not need to learn how to avoid contact nor how to escape the responsibility. What they need is to grow a mature ego, to establish their own worth. If I feel worthy as a person, I do not need to conquer, prove, or use people. I can then be tempted without the ego need pushing the temptation into lust.

Self-Worth

The issue, then, is not sex. The issue is self-worth. Until I have self-worth, I will need to prove. As long as I need to prove, I will need to use people for the proving. If I do not need to use people for the proving, I can handle the normal experiences of being tempted. When the temptation comes, I can think of the other person instead of being dominated by my own needs.

How Does God Help Us with Lust?

God goes behind the lust to the real need. He helps us feel worthy. He allows us to feel love and purpose, and worth. When this process is begun, we have done the proving, or we have at least begun doing the proving to ourselves instead of to others. When the proving is reduced, so is the need for sacrificing others in the process.

This may not sound as dramatic or as spiritual as "Jesus has won that battle," but it works. It is slow. It demands growth and time and struggle, but it works.

The victory in Jesus is self-worth—out of which everything else comes.

chapter ten

Self-Worth and Stress

There is a tree in west Texas which
leaned against the wind.
One day the wind did not blow—
the tree fell over.
I have lived in stress so long
if it stopped, I might fall apart.

I resigned from my job a couple of months ago. I had been a pastor for 30 years and was experiencing what psychologists call "burn-out." I took this step without any form of employment in mind. I had become convinced that I needed the challenge of finding new methods for communicating the gospel as I understand it.

It would be nice if I could report a great spiritual surge in my life that took away all fear and stress, but the truth is I am scared of the future and feel the stress which automatically accompanies fear. As I analyze my present feelings, there seem to be two kinds of stress: There is the stress of reality and the stress of fear.

The Stress of Reality

The stress of reality is the natural feelings which go with the reality of the situation. I have no job, no income, and no definite plans to count on. These things cause stress, and they *should* cause it. The stress I feel from this source is normal and natural and will only be handled by positive actions that will remove the source. This stress I can handle. No prayer meetings or spiritual experiences will make it all go away. I must deal with this stress on a reality level.

The Stress of Fear

The stress of fear is the reaction that comes from my own feelings of inadequacy. These are the feelings that make me wonder if I can handle the situation: Do I have the talent, the intelligence, the drive, and the organizational ability to succeed in my new endeavor? This kind of stress must be met on a different level than the stress of reality.

Dealing with Stress

The need to deal with stress should be self-evident. The results of stress are all around us. Doctors' offices are full of people with stress-related illnesses. Heart disease is still the number one killer, or, more accurately, *stress-caused* heart disease is the number one killer. Doctors now call high blood pressure *hypertension*, which indicates that there is a connection between blood pressure and stress.

Where does all of this stress come from? Why is there more stress now than ever before? It seems there should have been more stress during the Great Depression than there is now. The Great Depression was a time when thousands of people faced the problem of the stress of reality. They were out of work, broke, and there were no jobs. I often think we laughed our way through the Depression. Now we are depressing our way through prosperity. It does not make sense.

But it does make sense. Life was simpler then. Everyone was broke, so no one was under the gun to excel. There was the stress of reality, but the stress of fear was not as prevalent because the stress of fear comes from the pressure to perform and succeed. When this pressure comes, it brings feelings of inadequacy with it. Now that we have the Joneses to live up to, we tend to feel the stress of our own capabilities or lack of capabilities.

Because there are two kinds of stress, there must be a dual approach to dealing with the problem. We must deal with the stress of reality *and* the stress of fear.

ACCEPTANCE

The key word in dealing with the stress of reality is *acceptance*. The thing to avoid is the "feeling bad because we feel bad" syndrome. We have a thought or a feeling, then we think we should not think or feel this way, and we end up thinking there is something wrong with us or else we would not feel this way. The result is a snowball effect that convinces us we are crazy, or bad, or not Christians. This is the "feeling bad because we feel bad" syndrome.

We avoid this syndrome by acceptance. Someone said the paradox of life is that we only change after we accept ourselves. Until we accept ourselves, we spend all of our energies fighting against our own feelings.

Giving Permission. If we face real stress, the best thing to do is give ourselves permission to hurt, worry, and be depressed. These are real feelings responding to a real situation: No amount of kicking ourselves will make them go away. Kicking ourselves will only seem to intensify the feelings.

Dealing with the stress of reality is accomplished by telling ourselves we are worried and we *should* be worried. Then we must fight off the urge to worry about our worrying.

FEAR

Most of the stress we feel does not come from the stress of reality, but from the fears within us.

The stress of fear comes from the feelings we have that make us feel inadequate for the living we are called upon to do. If we feel inferior, then stress is a natural result. If we feel destined to fail we create a self-fulfilling prophecy of failure. When we are waiting for the failure to come, we wait in stress.

I have a dear friend who decided long ago that sooner or later something would happen that could not be handled. This friend's prophecy is that someday he will be overwhelmed. It is easy to see the stress caused by this feeling.

Stress, then, is the result of the fear of failure, the fear of rejection, or the fear of hurt.

How the Gospel Can Help

If the gospel is to help us in stress, it must work on the fears which create the stress. I could preach every Sunday on the sin of worry. I could create a great guilt trip for folks by telling them that God is not pleased when they worry. The result this preaching would produce is that folks would be worried about their worry.

I could preach about faith being the opposite of worry and make folks fear for their salvation. I could manipulate them into various religious experiences designed to make it all go away. I could capitalize on the fear and lead them to great activity and sacrificial giving to prove they are people of faith.

But none of these methods will work because they avoid dealing with the root of the problem. If people feel inadequate for living the life they are in, then those feelings of inadequacy must be met.

Affirmation

The key word in dealing with the stress of fear is *affirmation*. People need to be affirmed: They need to feel loved as human beings and to feel accepted as persons.

The Carrot-on-a-Stick Principle. We have trouble with affirmation though. We seem to feel that if people are affirmed they will never change. Our concept of change is based on the carrot-on-a-stick idea. If the carrot is held just out of reach of a horse, the horse will run after the carrot and pull the cart, but if the horse ever reaches the carrot, he will stop and never go again. Based on this concept, we withhold praise and affirmation, hoping people will keep running after the "carrot."

God has never used the carrot-on-a-stick principle. While we were yet sinners He died for us. The birth of Jesus was anything but a carrot on a stick. Long before man turned to God He sent His Son into the world. He did not wait for us to deserve the gift of His presence. Bethlehem was God's throwing the carrot into our midst before we ever ran after it.

God even used affirmation on His Son. At the Baptism of Jesus, before Jesus ever preached a sermon, performed any miracles, or even declared His Sonship, God affirmed Him.

As the baptism was completed, the dove appeared and the voice of God said, "This is My beloved Son." No wonder Jesus could go into the mountain to face temptation. The affirmation of God was ringing in His ears.

Jesus used affirmation on the people He met. He changed Simon's name to Peter, which meant rock. He called Peter a rock while he was still putty. The result of this affirmation turned Peter into a rock. He loved the woman at the well while she was still an outcast and a social misfit. John referred to himself as the disciple whom Jesus loved. These are the results of affirmation.

After 20 years as a counselor, I am convinced that the greatest need of us all is the feeling of being at peace with ourselves. To feel we are understood, accepted, and acceptable is the basic need we all experience and the place we all need to be. To be able to say, "I am me, and I have a right to be me," is the beginning of health.

FEELING AT PEACE WITH OURSELVES

We do not feel at peace from fear and guilt, from performance for God's love, nor from reading self-help books. The only way I know how to feel it is through the affirmation of God. We need to discover for ourselves the awesome truth of His love for us.

I wish I could offer you some kind of quick religious experience that would establish affirmation in you once and for all. But there is no quick fix. Affirmation is a process beginning with an initial discovery that God loves us— warts and all. This discovery may be in our conscious mind a long time before it becomes real to us on an emotional level. During this process we will experience many set- backs: There will be times when we feel loved, but also times when we feel unlovable. Let the process continue, and we gradually begin to know on an emotional level that we are accepted and loved by God.

Loving Ourselves

When we begin to feel affirmed, we also begin to love our- selves. If God can love us, maybe we can love also. Out of this process we begin to feel secure, and out of this secur- ity we begin to notice less feelings of inadequacy: those feelings of rejection, failure, and hurt.

One day we will look back and realize we no longer feel the same tension we once felt. Stress has been met not by working on the stress, but by healing the insecurity that created the stress in the first place.

chapter eleven

Self-Worth
and Selfishness

**Lord, all I ask out of life
is the right to show how much I can give,
After I am rich.**

Most of the problems I deal with in counseling could be called out-of-control selfishness. Boil down most of the big words we counselors use, and the result will be a self that cannot be handled. A paranoid person is someone who is totally dominated by the self. All that matters to such a person is how they are seen, treated, or threatened. Psychologists talk a great deal about ego: *Ego* is another word for being dominated by our own needs. When a person turns inward, they are turning toward illness: The more intense the turning, the more intense the illness.

REAL LIVING

The most practical words I have ever read come from the lips of Jesus. He said, "If you want to save your life, lose it." This theme is recorded nine times in the New Testament. It is verbalized in various ways, such as the "first must be last," or "give and you will receive"; but the theme is the same. Jesus was saying that real living happens when we break the domination of our own needs. His statement sounds like a paradox—die to live, lose to keep, or give to get. The statement sounds contrary to good sense, and is certainly contrary to human nature. After years of counseling, I must report the statement is not a paradox nor contrary to good sense. Rather, this statement is the healthiest and most completely true evaluation of life I have ever found.

SELFISHNESS

The reason the statement of Jesus has so much meaning for me is I have never known a selfish person who was happy: They are too busy in the desperate struggle to meet their own needs to be able to enjoy the world they are in. No matter what is going on, they are testing the wind to see how it affects them. Since they are looking for slights, hurts, rejections, and bad results, they find them all.

Selfish people look at every event in relation to how it affects them. They cannot rejoice when others are happy because they are only interested in their own happiness. They cannot feel when others hurt because they are dominated by their own hurt.

The selfish person is so dominated by his own situation that he cannot see the situation of anyone else. I have known people who, if they had walked into one of the extermination camps after World War II, would have looked around and said, "You think *these* people have troubles— let me tell you how bad the train ride was getting here." That may sound farfetched, but it isn't.

Domination

Selfish people are dominated by their own needs. They have so much left to prove that they become desperate: Every event must be used to get attention for themselves. They feel if they can get enough attention, they may one day find peace. They cannot meet their own needs, so they spend their lives demanding that everyone else meet them. Since the ultimate proving must come from within themselves, they fight a losing battle. When they lose, the needs become even more intense to compensate for the loss so they redouble their efforts and become even more dominated and, therefore, more selfish. Selfishness becomes an endless spiral going deeper and deeper into domination.

THE SELF

Jesus spoke of the concept of the self more often than He spoke of almost any other subject. He said more about saving by losing, getting by giving, and living by dying than

He did about Heaven, Hell, or the second coming. This concept is the basic idea of His new look at life.

The question is: How? How do we stop being selfish? What brings this dramatic transformation into our lives?

How to Cure Selfishness

Too often our approach to the "How?" tends to make matters worse instead of better. Too often we have tried to cure selfishness by making people feel guilty because of their selfishness. When guilt does not work, we try fear. Fear is probably the root cause of selfishness in the first place. Adding fear to selfishness is like trying to put out a fire with gasoline.

Guilt.   Guilt is applied to selfishness when we intimate that God is not pleased with us unless we are unselfish. If the emphasis is placed on pleasing God, then we are left with more of a struggle. As we struggle, we end up feeling more insecure. We compare ourselves with others and suffer by the comparison.

Control.   If we try to cure selfishness by control, we end up even more selfish. We cannot control selfishness unless we can see our own selfish acts. The only way we can see our selfishness is to spend a great deal of time looking at ourselves. This self-examination causes us to think more about ourselves while trying to reduce the time spent in self-interest.

Someone has called this the *me* generation. A trip to any bookstore will justify this title: The shelves are full of self-help books. A majority of the better selling books are "how to" books: How to get your way; how to win; how to get anything you want in twenty minutes. I call this the "How to be successfully selfish" or "How to be selfishly successful." There is no end of the making of books. There is also no end to the unhappiness and misery in our world. Evidently the books aren't doing much for us.

A DILEMMA

So we have a great dilemma. On the one hand, the gospel says we cannot be happy until we find a cure for selfishness. On the other hand, no one seems to be able to help us find a cure. About all we have received from the church are feelings of guilt and fear because we are selfish. So what *is* the answer? How do we find help?

Looking Behind Selfishness

As in the case of lust, anger, and stress, we must look behind the selfishness and find the root cause. If we can do so we can treat the disease instead of the symptoms. Selfishness is a symptom of the disease; it is not the disease.

We are selfish because we *need* to be—not because we *want* to be. There are very few selfish people in the world, but there *are* a lot of people who have so many needs they cannot focus on anything except their own needs. These people act and feel selfish. These acts and feelings are the result of needs not being met. They are not the willful acts and decisions of mean people.

We all have an instinct for survival. When we feel threatened, we act on the instinct to survive. If a building is on fire, our first reaction is to save ourselves. When we are surviving we are selfish. We have all heard stories of prisoners of war turning on each other over scraps of food: They were forced to live on the survival level. Survival level living is automatically selfish.

The Survival Level

The issue is: What causes so many of us to live on the survival level? Most of us have not found anything that will lift us above this level. It may be that more of us are trying to survive now than during other periods of history. We seem to feel a sense of desperation in our lives. It may be the threat of the atom bomb, the unrest in our world, the economic situation, the bad advice and the bad preaching we have been raised with. Whatever the cause, there seems to be a plague of survival going on.

It must be said that all of us revert to survival levels at some time in our lives. None of us is confident enough to avoid lapses. When we are threatened, we react instinctively. All of us, then, will be selfish at times. This is a normal aspect of life. We do not, however, have to live day-to-day on this level. There is hope for a higher ground of existence.

What causes the survival level? It is not really the times we live in. The times we live in are also a symptom, not the disease. The root causes are:

Fear.   The feeling that something is wrong with us is the basis for the fear. Most of us feel we are not alright. We think we are the only ones who feel the way we feel, think what we think, and respond as we respond. We think we are odd. The longer I live, the more I believe we are all pretty much alike. None of us are super-humans: None of us are above bad thoughts, bad feelings, and bad reactions. The problem is that we do not realize this. We have been programmed to think others are okay, but we are not okay. This fear leads to:

Competition.   We are in a life or death struggle with others. They are better than we are. We worry about what they think, what they say, and what they will do. We go to church and think everyone there is a better Christian than we are—somehow "they" have something we do not have. I often think the "super Christians" have done us more harm than the "carnal Christians." The very fact that we call some Christians "carnal Christians" proves my point. The super Christians make the rest of us feel like spiritual peons—they seem to have God's private, unlisted phone number while we get a busy signal or a recording. This makes even our religion become part of the problem instead of the solution. This leads to:

Pressure.   We feel we must perform to a high standard, but somehow we fail. The result is we intensify our fight with ourselves. The intensifying forces us to survival levels. The survival results in selfishness.

If we are to cure selfishness, we must find some way to focus on something other than our own needs. So we can live on another level. We must finally prove to ourselves that we are okay. If we can prove that, we can put ourselves to rest and worry about others. If we can't prove this, we will never put ourselves to rest.

A few years ago there was a best selling book called *I'm Okay, You're Okay.*[1] The book did a great job of explaining the problem: It outlined the causes of our "no okayness;" It dealt with the tapes we play in our minds; It traced the results of this program. Then the book stopped. It offered no way to change our ways. It explained the problem, but did not give the cure.

[1] Thomas A. Harris, M.D., *I'm OK-You're OK*, New York, Harper and Row, 1969.

SELF-WORTH AND GOD

I believe self-worth begins with God. I believe self-worth from God is the one power we need to change our focus from our own needs. If God—the being of ultimate worth—can help me discover His feelings of my worthiness, then I can begin to discover solid worth. Solid worth is the worth from within myself as opposed to worth which depends on the opinions of others. Discovering this worth is a slow process, but it becomes unshakable once it is found.

If we feel worth from within, it is hard to make us live on a survival level. The fear of others will no longer be as intense or as much of a problem. If God likes us and we develop a like for ourselves *based on* His liking us, then we can take it if others do not like us.

The result is we have only two people to please: We will please God and we will please ourselves. If we are pleasing to God and pleasing to ourselves but someone else does not find us pleasing, then they have a problem. *We* don't have a problem; *they* do.

The result is our fears are diminished and we are not as susceptible to mere survival. If we are not as susceptible to survival, we are also not as selfish. The proving is over, the defense is no longer needed, the competition is no longer relevant, and we can begin to live on a higher level.

The victory in Jesus is self-worth out of which everything else comes.

chapter twelve

Fine Wine Takes Time

I have spent 50 years
waiting expectantly for
overnight success.

The church seems to be addicted to what could be called "The Damascus Road Complex." The concept is Saul walking along a road to Damascus, seeing a blinding light, being blind for three days, getting baptized, and behold— he is an instant Apostle Paul. We seem to feel if God does something, it must be miraculous and instantaneous. If someone is healed in a dramatic display of power, then God did it. If someone is healed gradually through the processes of medicine and the body's own healing powers, then it is not a miracle of God.

Saul did not become Paul on the road to Damascus. He began the process there, but there *was* a process. He went to Arabia for a period of time, then he made tents in Tarsus where he became the Apostle Paul. It was not instantaneous: It took time, and struggle, and false starts. Fine wine takes time, and so do we.

MIRACLES VERSUS PROCESSES

Jesus seemed intent on getting people off the miracle kick. It was evident to Him that the major attraction they felt was the excitement of the instant healing. Again and again He confronted them with this fact. He often asked the one healed not to tell of the event and told the crowd that they followed only because of the miracles. He saw the danger of decisions to follow Him based on the excitement of miracles.

God has always been a God of process. He seems to have plenty of time to wait for the development of His people. How long did He wait for Abraham to develop faith? How long did He wait for Moses to develop courage and commitment? He waited 30 years for His own Son.

The idea of process in development will be tough to sell in our world. We want everything to be instant because we have done a good job of producing the instant: We have instant entertainment with the flip of a TV dial; we have instant meals, instant coffee, and instant transportation. Our lives are filled with the convenience of "quick."

The Quick World and Religion

Religion has adapted itself to this quick world. The major emphasis heard now is, "Come get a quick fix from God. He can heal your bodies, answer your questions, meet your needs, change your life, and, best of all—He can do it quickly. Just get saved, born again, converted, surrendered to God, on fire for God, or right with God—and all will be well."

The results of this are disastrous. We run folks through the emotional experiences of the faith and turn them loose with the expectation that their Damascus Road will produce the instant change of a Saul into a Paul. The folks expect the same. When the newness wears off, they find themselves faced with many of the problems they faced before. The problems are the same, but their relationship to the problems has changed. Now they are not supposed to have problems; the presence of problems means they have failed; they are in a fellowship of people who expect and demand that they have no problems. The result is a great deal of self-hate and disillusionment. More people drop out of Christianity because of disillusionment than for any other cause.

The Christian Process

Christianity is not instant. Christianity is a process. It may have a sudden beginning, but the beginning is just that—a beginning. Conversion is a birth; the living comes later.

129

The concepts of this book are a process. I know of no instant experience that will make us know the love of God in us. The past programming we have known is enough to make this a slow process. We do not get over our raising in a hurry. The good news is we *have* the time: We have our lifetime to spend digging deeper and deeper into the love of God and the person we are. We will never have it down pat: There will be ups and downs, times of assurance, and times of doubt—but through them all there is the slow process of growth.

The Better Product.   I am glad it is a process—glad because "process" always produces a better product than "instant." I think the better product is the rationale behind the plan of God. He could change us in an instant. There is no shortage of power in God. He could make it all so easy. Instead of quick and easy, He chose slow and hard. I think He made this choice for several reasons.

CREATING A CHRISTIAN

He is Trying to Build Us

One of the great theological questions is, "Does God want us to be holy or whole?" What is His plan? If we gave ourselves to Him fully, what kind of people would we be? Most of the time our answer to this question would be, "He wants us to be holy." The spirit of the New Testament says He is interested in our becoming whole people—He wants us to grow in *all* aspects of our lives. Just as Jesus grew physically, mentally, socially, and spiritually, we are to develop in the same areas. The goal of God is wholeness.

Wholeness does not come in a quick infusion of an outside force nor in a sudden turn-around. We *grow* toward wholeness. Christianity is addition, not subtraction. He does not come in to take away our past, our hangups, or even our faults. He adds Himself to us just as we are, and we begin to walk together. As we walk we come to know and understand each other and as we know and understand, we move closer to one another. The result is a process of change—a process that demands time.

He is Trying to Develop Us

Any growth is slow. The growth of personhood is very slow. There are several reasons for this growth's being slower than other forms of growth.

It is slow because it is frightening; in fact, any change is frightening. Changes inside ourselves are especially frightening: We feel as though we have thrown the baby out with the bath water; we think we have gone too far, that we have lost our direction, that we have lost our faith. The result is that we move one silly millimeter forward and two back, then one forward and one back. Finally, we begin to make progress.

Growth is slow because of its natural process. We grow in tension. When counseling people, I have to remember that no one can be helped until they *want* to be helped. Most of the time we do not want to be helped until we hurt. I must wait for folks to get ready to grow before I can do much with them in a counseling situation. This is true in all forms of growth: When tension comes or struggle hits, we grow. When the tension is eased, we hit a plateau and wait for the next tension. Because of the need for tension, growth is a slow process of spurt, stop, and spurt again. Our discovery of the love of God will fit this same process. We will grasp an inkling of His love, then wait for the next struggle to force us deeper. It takes a lifetime—on purpose.

He is Trying to Lead Us to Commitment

A young man began attending a church where I was pastor. He had always tried to be a God-pleaser: His concept of religion had always been one of demand and guilt. My style of preaching bothered him because he felt there were no demands put upon him—and he needed that. He was ready to quit until he made a discovery one Sunday morning. He related the discovery this way: "I thought this church was soft and weird. I felt there were no demands. Then one Sunday I realized I was being given the ultimate demand: It was being demanded that I do it myself."

Conformity and Commitment. There is a vast difference between conformity and commitment. Conformity is the mere yielding to pressure. Commitment is choice made on preference. If all God wanted from us was conformity, the task would be easy and quick. If God wants commitment, then the process is not easy and certainly not quick. Commitment comes from the depths of soul struggle. It happens gradually as we face life and gamble ourselves with choices. There is no quick way to make these gambles.

On the surface, this book seems to offer cheap grace. Find the love of God for yourself—no pressure, no guilt, no fear. It sounds easy and cheap, but it is neither. This is tough grace: It demands choices based on what is preferred; betting our life on the "Jesus Way" of being; thinking and digging and struggling until we know who we are and where we are going; and our dealing with ourselves and with others on a deeper level than the norm. There is nothing cheap or easy about the struggle of a soul.

He is Trying to Give Us Purpose

I do not believe in reincarnation. Once is enough for me, thank you. There is one concept of reincarnation I like and wish we could adopt: that is the view of purpose this theory gives. What if we are here more than once and the purpose of our being here is to see how far we can grow on this trip? That makes the purpose of living change from "What can I accomplish?" to "What can I become?" I think *becoming* is the purpose. God is trying to get us to see and the goal is how far we can grow. The growth is to become like Jesus. He is the model we follow—to feel like, see like, walk like, talk like, and love like Jesus. If this could become our purpose, the whole of our lives would change. If this could be our purpose, then value systems, relationships, attitudes, and activities would all be seen in a different perspective. If I think I am here to do, then I spend my time and energy doing. If I think I am here to become, then I get excited about changing and becoming.

Becoming

Becoming is the purpose of God. Everything else is a sounding gong or a crashing cymbal. Being like fine wine takes time.

There is, then, no magic formula to make this book work. There is no instant experience to make it real. We will know the facts in our heads a long time before we feel them in our experience. This is no invitation to a quick change; rather, it is an invitation to a slow struggle, to a process of discovering the love of God, and to a process of letting the love of God for us lead us to love others. I cannot say it will be quick, but I can say it will work. Self-worth is the victory in Jesus out of which everything else comes. Shall we begin?

Index

Conformity, 19, 21
and commitment, 132-33

D

"Damascus Road Complex," 127
Dependency on God, 70-71, 73
God's intentions, 70
Depression, 76, 84, 85-86, 87
stress, 107-8
Domination, 117
"Don't do that approach" to
preaching, 8-10

E

Ego need:
selfishness, 115
and temptation, 99-100
Emperor's new clothes, story of, 6-7
Experiences, personal, purpose, 54
Ezekiel, 48-49

F

Faith, 5, 29, 74, 75, 109, 131
Fear:
anger, 87
of failure, 109
of God, 28
guilt, 10-11, 12
lust, 94
of others, 123
selfishness, 119
sex, 95
stress, 105-9
survival level living, 121
Feeling at peace, 111-12
Female sex drive, 100
"Five easy steps" method of
preaching, 11
Focus weeks, religious, 59
buzz sessions, 59-63
Forgiveness, 64
Frustration, 29, 30
Fulfillment, human, 17

G

Getting God to love us, 29-31, 33-41
behavior/misbehavior, 35-37, 38-40
unconditional love of God, 40
Gospel:
power of, 22
selling, 8
stress, 109-10
Grace, 37-38, 133
falling into, 29, 31
Great Depression, 107
Greed, 16, 40
Grief, 64
Growth, personal, 73-74
healing, 75-78
personhood, 131-32
Guilt:
and fear, 10-11, 12
religion, 132
selfishness, 118, 119
and self-worth, 64-65
worry, 109

H

Hate, 52
Healing:
miracles, 128
self-responsibility, 74-78
Heart disease, and stress, 106
Hebrews, 97
How Christ answers, 5-12
Hypertension, 106

I

I'm OK–You're OK, 122
Incompetency, emphasis on in Christian
sermons, 70-71
Independent thinking, 73-74
Inferiority, 20, 26-30, 54, 77
stress, 108
Insecurity, 20, 112
female sex drive, 100
guilt, 118
and problem tempers, 88
Isaiah, 50

Stress, 105-12, 119
  acceptance, 107-8
  affirmation, 110-12
  feeling at peace, 111-12
  of reality and fear, 105-6, 107, 108-9
  "Super Christians," 121-22
Survival level living, 120-23

T

Teasing, harm of, 27
Tempers, problem, 84, 88-89
  control, 89
  insecurity, 88-89
Temptation, and lust, 96-99

female sex drive, 100
  male sex drive, 99
Truth, 74

V

Virgin birth, 49

W

War, 16
Wisdom and insight, 72-73
Witnessing, 35, 39
Worrying, 10
  as sin, 109